Searchlight
BOOKS™

How Does
Your Body
Work?

Your
Muscular
System

Rebecca L. Johnson

Lerner Publications Company
Minneapolis

For Mum

Lerner Publications Company
A division of Lerner Publishing Group, Inc.
241 First Avenue North
Minneapolis, MN 55401 U.S.A.

Website address: www.lernerbooks.com

Library of Congress Cataloging-in-Publication Data

Johnson, Rebecca L.
      Your muscular system / by Rebecca L. Johnson.
          p.   cm. — (Searchlight books™—how does your body work?)
      Includes index.
      ISBN 978–0–7613–7449–7 (lib. bdg. : alk. paper)
         1. Musculoskeletal system—Juvenile literature. I. Title.
      QP301.J586 2013
      612.7—dc23   2011044166

Manufactured in the United States of America
1 – DP – 7/15/12

Contents

Chapter 1

BODY MOVERS

Every time you take a step, blink your eyes, or smile, you can thank your muscles. Muscles make you move. Some movements are large. You leap over a puddle. You swing a bat. Other movements are small. You raise an eyebrow. You tap your finger.

What do muscles make it possible for you to do?

You can see some muscles at work. Try "making a muscle" with your arm. Can you see the muscle bulging just under your skin?

You can't see other muscles in your body. When you swallow, muscles push food into your stomach. Muscles in the stomach wall mix your food. Muscles in your heart move blood through your body.

You can see some muscles just under your skin.

Muscles help you do all the things you do.

Working with Other Systems

You need your muscles for almost everything you do. So it's not surprising that you have hundreds of them. All these muscles make up your muscular system. The muscular system works with other body systems to keep you alive and healthy. It helps you do all the things you do.

Muscle Control

You can control some muscles. You can make them move just by thinking. Suppose you want to pick an apple. You reach out and curl your fingers around the apple. You pull it down. You decide you want to do this. And your muscles make it happen.

WHEN YOU PICK AN APPLE, YOU USE MUSCLES YOU CAN CONTROL.

There are other muscles that you cannot control, no matter how hard you try. You can't make food travel to your stomach more quickly. You can't make your heart beat more slowly. These kinds of muscles do their work automatically.

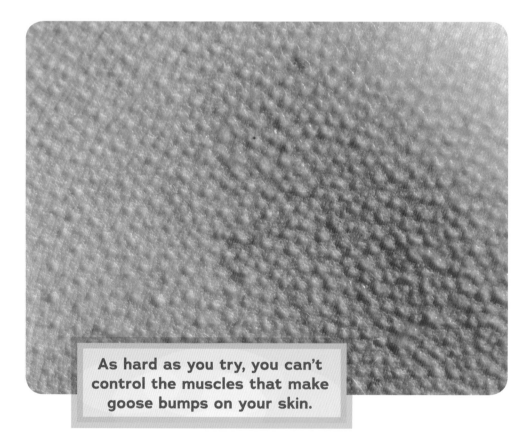

As hard as you try, you can't control the muscles that make goose bumps on your skin.

Contracting Muscles

All muscles are alike in one important way. They all can contract, or shorten. When a muscle contracts, it moves whatever body part it's attached to. You can see muscles contract in your arm. The big muscle in your upper arm is called the biceps. When your biceps contracts, your lower arm moves up.

Put your right hand on your left biceps. Bend your left elbow. Can you feel your biceps contracting as your lower arm moves up?

Chapter 2

HOW MUSCLES WORK

Muscles move body parts by contracting. But how do muscles contract?

Muscles are made up of cells. Each muscle cell is called a muscle fiber. A muscle fiber is thinner than one of the hairs on your head.

Muscles are made up of many muscle fibers. How big are muscle fibers?

Strands

Inside each muscle fiber are hundreds of strands. These strands are made up of even thinner strands. The thinnest strands overlap one another. They look like fingers laced together.

The thinnest strands of muscle fiber overlap like fingers laced together.

Nerves

Your brain controls your body. It sends messages all the time. These messages go to every part of your body. They travel along nerves. Nerves reach into every muscle. They touch every muscle fiber.

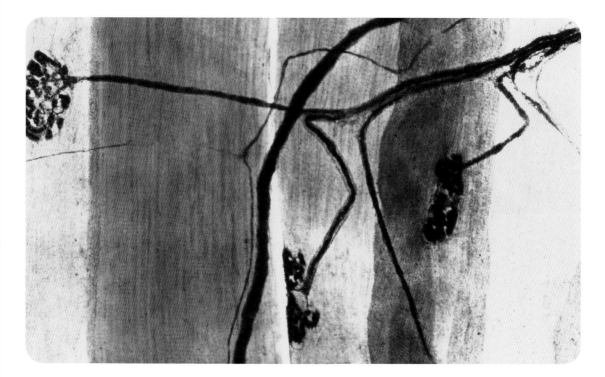

NERVES CARRY MESSAGES TO MUSCLE FIBERS.

When a message reaches a muscle fiber, the tiny strands inside it move. The strands slide toward one another. So the muscle fiber gets shorter.

As muscle fibers get shorter, the whole muscle contracts. It pulls on the body parts that it is attached to. It makes the body parts move.

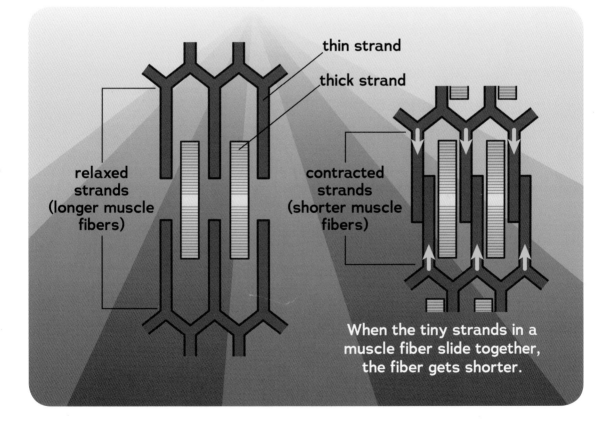

thin strand

thick strand

relaxed
strands
(longer muscle
fibers)

contracted
strands
(shorter muscle
fibers)

When the tiny strands in a
muscle fiber slide together,
the fiber gets shorter.

Chapter 3

MUSCLES YOU MOVE

You have three different kinds of muscles in your body. All three kinds are made up of muscle fibers that contract. But each kind of muscle does a special job.

Skeletal muscles are all over your body. Can you name one of your skeletal muscles?

Skeletal Muscles

Muscles that you control are called skeletal muscles. The biceps is a skeletal muscle. Skeletal muscles have long, thin muscle fibers. Under a microscope, the fibers look striped.

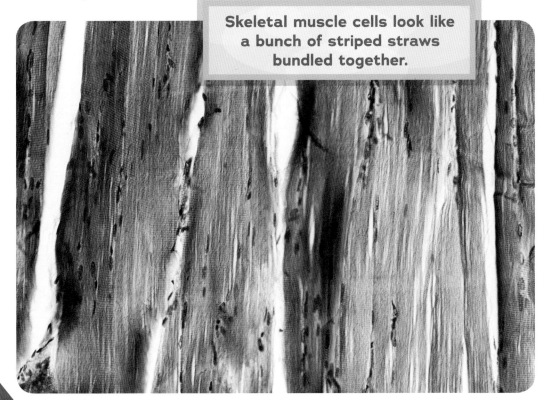

Skeletal muscle cells look like a bunch of striped straws bundled together.

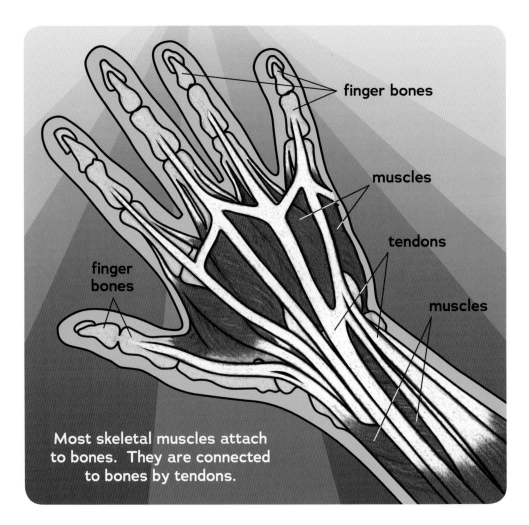

finger bones

muscles

tendons

muscles

finger bones

Most skeletal muscles attach to bones. They are connected to bones by tendons.

Most skeletal muscles are attached to bones. When the muscles contract, they pull on the bones where they are attached. Your bones cannot move without the help of muscles.

Tendons

Tendons connect muscles to bones. Look at the back of your hand. Try wiggling your fingers. Do you see the cords moving just under your skin? Those cords are tendons. They connect muscles in your lower arm to your finger bones.

TENDONS CONNECT MUSCLES TO BONES. WIGGLE YOUR FINGERS. YOU CAN SEE YOUR TENDONS MOVE.

Muscle Pairs

No bone can move without the help of a muscle. But muscles can only pull. They cannot push. That's why many skeletal muscles come in pairs. One muscle pulls a bone in one direction. Then the other muscle pulls the bone in the opposite direction.

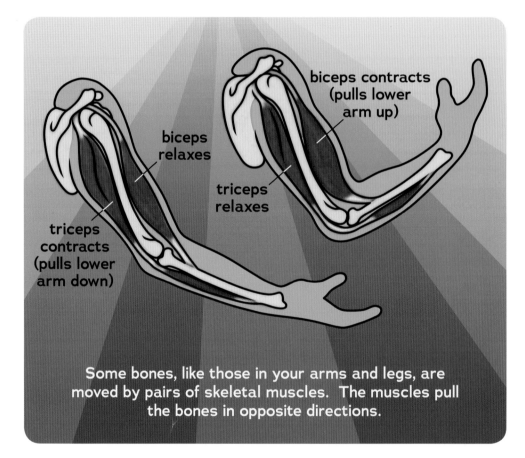

biceps contracts
(pulls lower
arm up)

biceps
relaxes

triceps
relaxes

triceps
contracts
(pulls lower
arm down)

Some bones, like those in your arms and legs, are moved by pairs of skeletal muscles. The muscles pull the bones in opposite directions.

Your biceps and triceps muscles pull in opposite directions to move your lower arm up and down.

In your upper arm, your biceps is paired with a muscle called the triceps. These muscles are attached to bones in your lower arm and your shoulder. When your biceps contracts, your lower arm is pulled up. When your triceps contracts, your lower arm is pulled down.

Most movements need more than just two muscles. More than three hundred muscles work together when you take a single step!

Many skeletal muscles in your face are attached to your skin. Nearly one-fourth of all the skeletal muscles in your body are in your face.

Not all skeletal muscles are attached only to bones. Some are attached to other muscles. Some are attached to skin.

Skeletal muscles attached to skin on your face can raise an eyebrow. Others can pull the corners of your mouth up into a smile.

Muscle Shapes and Sizes

Skeletal muscles come in all sorts of shapes and sizes. Big fan-shaped muscles are in your chest. They help move your arms at the shoulder. A flat sheet of muscle is just under your rib cage. It changes the shape of your chest to help you breathe.

Many skeletal muscles are large and powerful. They help you make big body movements.

The calf muscles in your lower legs are some of the strongest muscles in your body. They help you jump, walk, and run.

Your longest skeletal muscles are on the inside of your legs. They stretch from your hips to the insides of your knees. Thanks to these muscles, you can sit cross-legged!

The many different muscles in your legs help you move your legs in many different ways.

Smaller, less powerful skeletal muscles control body parts that move in small ways.

Hand and Eye Muscles

There are about twenty small muscles in your hands. With their help, you can make a fist. Or you can play the piano. Or you can pick up a dime.

Six muscles move each of your eyes. These muscles allow you to look in many directions. Keep your head still and look around. You can feel your eye muscles at work.

Skeletal muscles are powerful. But when they are working hard, they get tired quickly. Try squeezing a small rubber ball over and over again. Soon the muscles in your hand will start to hurt.

After a while, you won't be able to squeeze the ball even one more time. Your muscles are too tired to contract. Stop squeezing. Let the muscles in your hand rest. Soon they will be ready to work again.

When skeletal muscles contract over and over again, they quickly get tired. They need to rest before they can work again.

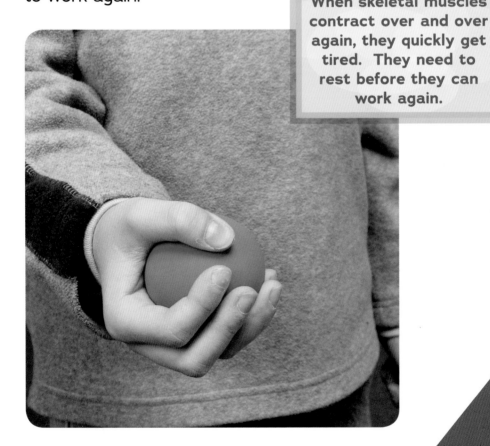

Chapter 4

MUSCLES THAT MOVE THEMSELVES

The second kind of muscle in your body is smooth muscle. Unlike skeletal muscle, you can't control smooth muscle. Smooth muscle contracts automatically. It contracts all by itself. That way, you don't have to think about things like digesting your food!

Smooth muscle is in blood vessels. Can you control smooth muscles?

Where Is Smooth Muscle?

Smooth muscle is found in the walls of your stomach. It is found in your blood vessels. It also makes up part of many organs in your body. When you are cold, tiny smooth muscles pull on the hairs in your skin. Then you get goose bumps!

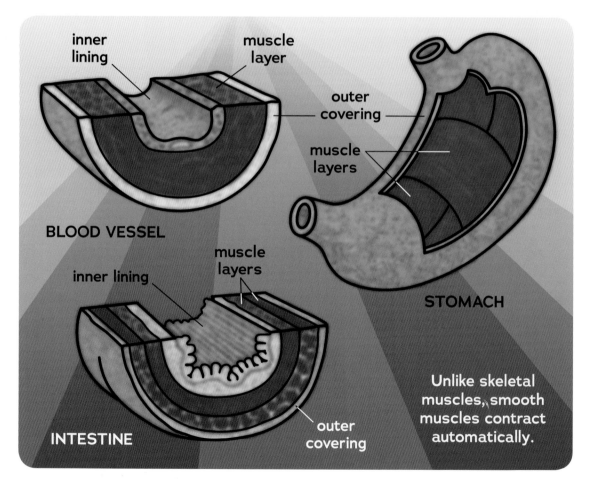

inner lining

muscle layer

outer covering

BLOOD VESSEL

muscle layers

STOMACH

inner lining

muscle layers

outer covering

INTESTINE

Unlike skeletal muscles, smooth muscles contract automatically.

Under a Microscope

Under a microscope, smooth muscle fibers look different from skeletal muscle fibers. They work differently too. Skeletal muscles can contract very fast. But smooth muscles contract slowly and steadily.

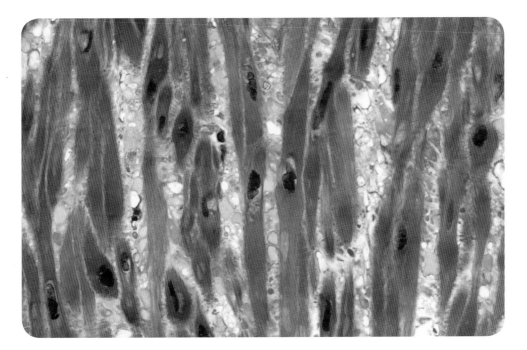

SMOOTH MUSCLE FIBERS ARE POINTED AT THE ENDS. THEY DON'T HAVE STRIPES AS SKELETAL MUSCLE FIBERS DO.

Smooth muscles are often arranged in flat sheets. A sheet of smooth muscle can stretch a lot! The smooth muscles in your stomach stretch so your stomach can hold a big meal.

YOUR STOMACH CAN HOLD A LOT OF FOOD BECAUSE THE SMOOTH MUSCLES IN THE STOMACH WALL CAN STRETCH.

Chapter 5

THE HEART

The third kind of muscle in your body is heart muscle. Heart muscle is found only in the walls of your heart. You can't control heart muscle. It contracts automatically. That's a good thing. You wouldn't want to have to think about every heartbeat!

Your heart muscle has been contracting since long before you were born. Where is heart muscle found?

Never Rests

Under a microscope, heart muscle looks a little bit like skeletal muscle. But it's different in an important way. Heart muscle never gets tired. It contracts about seventy times every minute. That's about one hundred thousand times a day. Heart muscle never rests during your entire life.

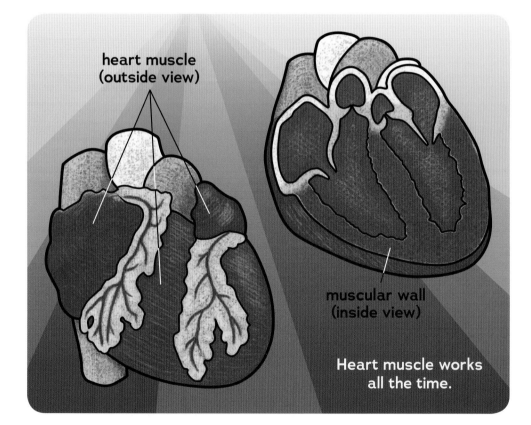

heart muscle
(outside view)

muscular wall
(inside view)

Heart muscle works
all the time.

Put your hand on the left side of your chest. Can you feel a thumping? That's your heart beating. With each beat, your powerful heart muscle contracts.

YOUR HEART MAKES A LUB-DUB, LUB-DUB SOUND AS IT BEATS. YOUR DOCTOR LISTENS TO THESE HEART SOUNDS WHEN YOU GET A CHECKUP.

Chapter 6

KEEPING MUSCLES HEALTHY

Each time your heart muscle contracts, it pumps blood out of your heart. The blood is pumped through your body. Blood carries nutrients to your body's cells. Nutrients feed cells. Some of those cells are muscle fibers.

Your heart pumps about 3,000 gallons (11,356 liters) of blood through blood vessels each day. Where does blood go?

Nutrients and Oxygen

Your body's cells need nutrients to work well. Nutrients come from the food you eat. Eating well helps keep your muscles healthy.

Blood also carries oxygen to your cells. You bring oxygen into your body with every breath. The harder your muscles work, the more oxygen they need.

Food gives your body the nutrients it needs.

Exercise

Hard work is good for muscles. Exercise doesn't give you more muscles. But the muscles you have get bigger and stronger.

WHEN YOU EXERCISE HARD, YOU BREATHE FASTER AND MORE DEEPLY. THIS BRINGS MORE OXYGEN INTO YOUR BODY.

Without exercise, muscles shrink. They lose their strength. Think about when you've been sick in bed for a long time. When you first start to walk again, your muscles feel weak.

When your arm is in a cast, you can't use your muscles. They get weak.

You probably don't think much about your muscles. But whether you're asleep or awake, your muscles are always working. At any one time, some muscles are contracting. Other muscles are relaxing. But they are all working together. Muscles make your body move in just the right way.

Your muscles work around the clock to keep you alive and healthy. They even work when you're asleep!

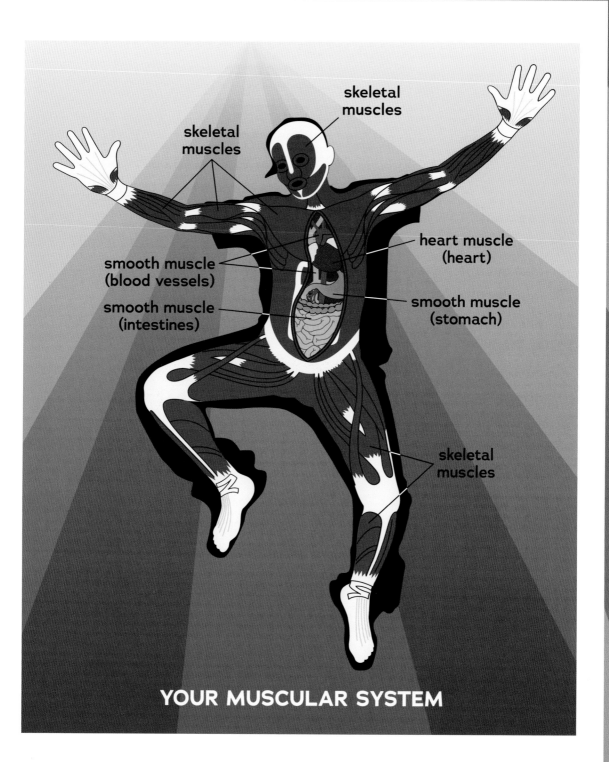

skeletal
muscles

skeletal
muscles

smooth muscle
(blood vessels)

smooth muscle
(intestines)

heart muscle
(heart)

smooth muscle
(stomach)

skeletal
muscles

YOUR MUSCULAR SYSTEM

Glossary

biceps: the muscle on the front of your upper arm

blood vessel: a tube in the body that carries blood

brain: a complex organ in the head that controls all body processes

cell: the smallest building block of body structures

contract: to shorten or pull together

heart muscle: the muscle in the heart. It contracts automatically.

microscope: a tool that makes very small things look bigger

muscle fiber: a muscle cell

nerve: a cell that carries messages between the brain and the rest of the body

nutrient: food for your cells

organ: a body part that has a special purpose. The lungs, the stomach, the liver, and the brain are organs.

oxygen: a gas that all cells need. It is carried in the blood.

skeletal muscle: muscle that you move

smooth muscle: muscle that contracts automatically

tendon: a tough band that connects muscles to bones

triceps: the muscle on the back of your upper arm

LERNER e SOURCE

Expand learning beyond the printed book. Download free, complementary educational resources for this book from our website, www.lerneresource.com.

Learn More about the Muscular System

Books

Burstein, John. *The Mighty Muscular-Skeletal System.* New York: Crabtree, 2009. Burstein takes a lively look at muscles and bones.

Green, Jen. *Muscles.* Mankato, MN: Stargazer Books, 2006. This title provides an introduction to how muscles work together to perform movements and tells what to eat to keep muscles healthy.

Stewart, Melissa. *Moving and Grooving: The Secrets of Muscles and Bones.* New York: Marshall Cavendish Benchmark, 2011. This book provides lots of fun facts about your muscles and bones.

Storad, Conrad J. *Your Circulatory System.* Minneapolis: Lerner Publications Company, 2013. Read about another important body system, the circulatory system, and find out how it works together with the muscular system to keep your body working well.

Websites

IMCPL Kids' Info Guide: Muscular System
http://www.imcpl.org/kids/guides/health/muscularsystem.html
This page from the Indianapolis Marion County Public Library has a list of resources you can use to learn more about the muscular system.

KidsHealth: Your Muscles
http://kidshealth.org/kid/htbw/muscles.html
This article offers a detailed explanation of the muscular system, and it's enhanced with sound and diagrams.

Welcome to Muscles
http://library.thinkquest.org/5777/mus2.htm?ttql-iframe
Click on the lizard for a tour of the whole muscular system.

Index

Photo Acknowledgments

The images in this book are used with the permission of: © Vito Palmisano/Photographer's Choice/Getty Images, p. 4; © Jon Feingersh/Blend Images/the Agency Collection/Getty Images, p. 5; © Stockbyte/Getty Images, p. 6; © Dan Kenyon/Taxi/Getty Images, p. 7; © Tyler Olson/ Dreamstime.com, p. 8; © Image Source/Getty Images, p. 9; © Marshall Sklar/Photo Researchers/ Getty Images, p. 10; © moodboard/Cultura/Getty Images, p. 11; © Biophoto Associates/Photo Researchers/Getty Images, pp. 12, 25; © Laura Westlund/Independent Picture Service, pp. 13, 14, 16, 18, 26, 30, 37; © age fotostock/SuperStock, p. 15; © Riderofthestorm/Dreamstime.com, p. 17; © Joos Mind/Stone/Getty Images, p. 19; © Brad Wilson/The Image Bank/Getty Images, p. 20; © Elena Nikolaeva/Cultura/StockImage/Getty Images, p. 21; © Buena Vista Images/Lifesize/Getty Images, p. 22; © Asia Images/SuperStock, p. 23; © Todd Strand/Independent Picture Service, p. 24; © G. W. Willis/Oxford Scientific/Getty Images, p. 27; © Jose Luis Pelaez Inc./Blend Images/Getty Images, p. 28; © Steve Gschmeissner/Photo Researchers, Inc., p. 29; © Sean Justice/Stone/Getty Images, p. 31; © Dr. Fred Hossler/Visuals Unlimited, Inc., p. 32; © Tetra Images/Getty Images, p. 33; © Ty Allison/Photographer's Choice/Getty Images, p. 34; © ERproductions Ltd./Blend Images/the Agency Collection/Getty Images, p. 35; © Joel Sartore/National Geographic/Getty Images, p. 36.

Front cover: © Cliparea/Custom media/Shutterstock.com.

Main body text set in Adrianna Regular 14/20
Typeface provided by Chank